RIGHT NOW PRAYERS

Revive your Faith and Unleash the Power of Praying in your Life

Mike Taylor

Rightnowprayers.com

No part of this book may be reproduced or transmitted in any form or by any means, electronic or mechanical, including recording, or by any information storage and retrieval system, without written permission from the publisher. The only exception is brief quotations in printed reviews. For more information, visit rightnowprayers.com.

Except where noted, scriptures are taken from the New King James Version. Copyright 1982 by Thomas Nelson, Inc. Used by permission. All rights reserved.

Table of Contents

INTRODUCTION 1

    PSALMS 121:1 "I WILL LIFT UP MINE EYES UNTO THE HILLS..." 5

ENCOURAGEMENT TO KEEP PRAYING 7

    PSALMS 51:10 "CREATE IN A CLEAN HEART, O GOD" 9

PRAYER FOR BREAKTHROUGH 11

    ISAIAH 30:41 "BUT THEY THAT WAIT UPON THE LORD SHALL RENEW THEIR STRENGTH..." 13

PRAYER FOR SELF ENCOURAGEMENT 15

PRAYER FOR PROSPERITY 17

    PHILIPPIANS 4:6 "BE ANXIOUS FOR NOTHING, BUT IN EVERYTHING BY PRAYER..." 19

PRAYER FOR CONTINUING TRUST 21

PRAYER FOR THE BEREAVED 23

PRAYER FOR EFFECTIVE WITNESS 27

    JAMES 5:16 - "THE EFFECTIVE, FERVENT PRAYER OF A RIGHTEOUS MAN..." 29

PRAYER AGAINST AN ATTACK FROM THE ENEMY 31

    CORINTHIANS 10:13 "THERE HATH NO TEMPTATION TAKEN YOU..." .. 33

A PRAYER FOR WEARY BELIEVERS 35

    Psalms 30:5 "Weeping may endure for a night..." 37

PRAYER IN THE MIDST OF TROUBLE 39

    Habakkuk 3:17 "Although the fig tree shall not blossom..." .. 40

PRAYER FOR PERSEVERANCE 41

PRAYER FOR ENDURING PERSONAL TRIALS 43

    Proverbs 12:4 "A virtuous woman is a crown to her husband" 46

PRAYER THAT OUR WITNESSING BE HEARD 47

    Proverbs 30: 8 - 9 "Remove falsehood and lies far from..." 49

PRAYER FOR SALVATION 50

PRAYER FOR HONORING GOD 52

    Psalms 73:25 - "Whom have I in heaven but you?" 54

PRAYER FOR MEN TO TAKE RESPONSIBILITY 55

    Matthew 11:29 - 30 "Take my yoke upon you, and learn of me..." 58

ENCOURAGEMENT TO BECOME A VIRTUOUS WOMAN 59

    Proverbs 31:10 "Who can find a virtuous woman?" 61

PRAYER FOR THOSE ABROAD 63

    Joshua 1:9 "Have I not commanded you?" 64

PRAYER FOR THE STRENGTH OF FRIENDS 65

MATTHEW 18:20 "FOR WHERE TWO OR THREE ARE GATHERED TOGETHER..." 68

PRAYER FOR SECURITY IN GOD 69

PRAYER FOR UNITY 71

PRAYER AND ADVICE CONCERNING MARRIAGE INFIDELITY .. 73

RUTH 3:11 - "AND NOW, MY DAUGHTER, FEAR NOT..." 81

PRAYER TO FORGIVE FAMILY MEMBER THEFT 82

PHILLIPIANS 4:7 "...AND THE PEACE OF GOD, WHICH SURPASSES ALL UNDERSTANDING..." 85

PRAYER FOR FAVOR IN COURT 86

ISAIAH 54:17 "NO WEAPON THAT IS FORMED AGAINST THEE SHALL PROSPER..." 88

PRAYER FOR SPIRITUAL CHANGE 89

ENCOURAGEMENT: SEEK THE "SON" AND LIVE! 91

1 CHRONICLES 16:34 "O GIVE THANKS UNTO THE LORD; FOR HE IS GOOD..." 93

ENCOURAGEMENT: FIGHTING A TROUBLING SPIRIT 95

ENCOURAGEMENT: IT WILL GET BETTER 99

ENCOURAGEMENT: YOUR TURN TO LOVE GOD 101

MATTHEW 18:3 "EXCEPT YE BE CONVERTED, AND BECOME AS LITTLE CHILDREN..." 102

PRAY AS OUR FATHER IN HEAVEN INSTRUCTS: HE KNOWS ALL THINGS 103

    ISAIAH 26:3 "THOU WILT KEEP HIM IN PERFECT PEACE..." 104

PRAYER FOR THE PREPARATION OF CHRIST'S RETURN 105

ABOUT THE AUTHOR AND MY HEALING TESTIMONIES 107

PERSONAL JOURNAL OF TESTIMONIES (JOT) 111

Introduction

Prayer changes things.

I don't know this by rumor; I know this by experience. Have you ever:

- Faced a tough situation and felt helpless about it?
- Had a hard time forgiving someone?
- Lacked support from family or friends?
- Felt like just giving up?

Well, I and many other Christians have had similar issues. But the good news is, God gives us answers when we *pray*.

In this inspirational prayer collection, you will be encouraged to know that people just like you are going through trials - and emerging victorious!

What makes this book different? These are real-life prayers for a **'right now** situation' from seasoned prayer warriors. It also includes images with power scriptures for additional encouragement.

To protect the privacy of group members, some of the names have been changed. However, I have kept the names of my wife, Kim, and my own.

When you read many of the prayers, you will feel as though they were written just for you. The prayers will revive your faith in God's ability to answer your prayers. You need this encouragement, especially when you can't see how God is working.

While I was praying, I remembered a powerful visit to my sister's house. Her youngest daughter was there with her newborn, who was less than a year old. He was sitting in his walker in a room adjacent to the kitchen crying. I asked her if he needed his diaper changed, but she said he was just hungry and she knew that without checking his diaper.

She got up to prepare his bottle as the child continued to cry. The child, from a different room, would follow her with his eyes as she moved back and forth in the kitchen preparing his bottle. But he continued to cry as if to say "Don't you hear me crying?" or "Why won't you answer or feed me?"

When she disappeared from his sight, he really started to cry and fuss as if he had lost all hope of being fed, and yet she silently continued to prepare his meal.

I felt sorry for him because I knew and saw as an outsider (angel to him) that his mom (godlike to him) was diligently working to get him what he needed, but the child did not understand this nor could he see his mom working to supply his necessity as she stepped out of his viewing range for the moment.

I picked the child up and he stopped crying long enough to look me over with a surprised look on his face as if to say "What?" and "Who are you?"

He looked me over, at my eyes, my nose, my lips and back to my eyes. Then he grabbed my nose and squeezed it while still looking me over. After his curiosity had waned and he realized he still needed food, he went back to howling again.

However, his mom was ready to give him his bottle and she came and took him from my arms. Without even looking at her, he immediately went passive because he recognized her touch and that alone was very soothing for him. When she gave him his bottle, his eyes seemed to roll back in his head; he was in heaven for he was being fed and in the arms of his mother.

I could easily see myself as the child, and because I know the mom is just like God to the infant, I can now truly wait without crying for my provision because I know my blessing is coming. Even when I don't see God, I know He is not far, just out of sight for the moment doing whatever He needs to do for my welfare.

I pray this message really lifts your spirit and I hope it has encouraged you too. Do you sometimes get impatient, wanting God to hurry up and deliver the wonderful vision he has shown you of your future? I know I sometimes do. You might be in that position **right now**, working on your many goals and waiting for the full benefits to manifest.

Two scriptures can help make the wait easier:

James 1:4: "But let patience have its perfect work, that you may be perfect and complete, lacking nothing (NKJV)."

Remind yourself that God wants to give you His absolute best and if your blessing is delayed, it is only because it will be better than you imagine!

Galatians 6:9: "And let us not grow weary while doing good, for in due season we shall reap if we do not lose heart (NKJV)."

Ask yourself this question: "What can I do **right now** to prepare myself for receiving this blessing?" Whatever it is, start doing that so that you can get maximum benefit and enjoyment from the blessing when it arrives.

While compiling this book, my soul was again blessed and refreshed as I remembered how God was faithful to answer our prayers.

You will also be able to review these prayers over and over again at different times as you walk in Christ - and be strengthened and encouraged once again. You will have a '**Right Now** Prayer' at your fingertips.

We are helpers one to another and this prayer book will indeed help you.

Yes, it is true that women tend to be the prayer warriors in a household. However, God still has praying men in the name of Jesus.

I am a praying man.

-Mike Taylor-

Psalms 121:1 "I will lift up mine eyes unto the hills..."

*I will lift up mine eyes unto the hills, from whence cometh my help.
My help cometh from the LORD, which made heaven and earth.
Psalms 121: 1 - 2 KJV*

Encouragement to Keep Praying

You have remembered Your people, Lord and for that we thank You.

I laid upon my bed one morning contemplating my day. I constructed a schedule of events from within and yet one thing was lacking in my itinerary which You have graciously reminded me of. I didn't intend to forego prayer, my Father, but I did indeed forget but for a moment.

Because You love Your people so and You desire to hear from us, You nudged me and I truly thank You for that because there are some who would rather I say nothing at all.

Yet I shall proclaim Your goodness throughout the land during good times, bad times and all times for You are worthy of praise and honor.

Be with me this day, Father as I go about with You on my mind and in my heart; but not me alone.

Be with my co-laborers as well as they journey through this one day. One day is all I am asking for now. Help us to get through this one day as victors and not victims. Help us to prosper in peace.

You have rewarded us many times according to our actions and yet You have gifted us with salvation according to Your love.

Now about the gift versus the reward. I will ask the age-old question: "Why would You gift us with anything?" The word *gift* backwards makes no sense (tfig) and yet the word reward (drawer) makes plenty of sense in that rewards seem to draw us close to You. I suppose one could use the T.F.I.G. as an acronym to mean "The Freedom In God" which is exactly what the "**Gift**" of salvation is.

Oh how great and wonderful You are to us and for us. We are indeed victors and we shall be **victorious** this day and everyday in Christ.

Now, we shall sing praises to You all the daylong from within and without.

We thank You Father for all things,

- Amen -

Mike Taylor

Psalms 51:10 "Create in a clean heart, O God"

Prayer for Breakthrough

We come before You Father in Heaven as a humble people, for we recognize Your awesome power and loving nature.

We are asking for You to continue to bear us up and help us to glorify You in our natural body, so that others may come to recognize how magnificent You are. Help us to not sin against You and most certainly we ask that You forgive us of our sins.

We have read in Genesis 32 where Jacob wrestled with the Angel for a blessing and protection. He believed his brother was hot on his heel and wanted to kill him for the evil he had done against his brother.

You knew he could not prevent You from leaving, but it appeared as though You wanted to see if he really wanted You and the blessing. So You touched the hollow of his thigh and knocked it out of joint since Jacob was so persistent.

In other words, Father, You gave Jacob a "Break"! We are persistent and we are asking for a break through You Father. We know that we shall heal stronger from Your break. We are asking for a break from our labor, but just for a moment so that we can exhale. We are asking for a break through our obstacles.

We ask for a "brake" for our loved ones to help them stop the downward spiral - to aid them in stopping the train wreck to which they may be headed. Help and strengthen us to be the "Brakeman" in our family and at our jobs. We need a break Father, yes, we need a "brake."

You know what type of break or brake we need:

* Break-up (the evil plans the enemy have for us)

* Break-out (of our slump and funk)

* Break-down (from pride)

* Break-through (barriers)

* Break-away (from our problems)

* Break-into praise unto You O'Lord

* Brake hard long enough to see Your salvation.

And when it is all said and done, we shall "Break-dance" unto Your goodness, for You are Good all the time and all the time You are good!

We do trust and love You Father!

~Amen~

Mike Taylor

Isaiah 30:41 "But they that wait upon the Lord shall renew their strength..."

Prayer for Self Encouragement

Majesty, we worship Your Majesty. Abba Father how wonderful You are. Thank You for Your faithfulness to us.

As Jesus called Peter to come to Him when He was on the water, Peter could do the impossible when he kept his eyes on Jesus. Father remind us this day that **nothing** is impossible and to believe You are able " to do exceedingly abundantly above **all** we can ask or think."

Dad, we remind You that Your Word declares "that You are not a man that You should lie nor the son of man that You should repent" (Numbers 23:19 KJV). Thank You that You are not double-minded, but what You declare **YOU** will do. We are excited about today. We don't know what this day holds, but we know who holds this day and that is good enough for us.

I have a thankful heart because I know what You have done for me. How You lovingly and patiently changed my life. To teach me that You are a good Father. My obedience to You is directly related to my relationship to You. You loved me when I obeyed and when I didn't and thought I knew better. You let me learn from my mistakes and that has helped me grow in my trust in You. That is why I know how much You love me. My heart breaks for those who have not experienced this awesome love.

I speak over our lives the Word that You put in my spirit. That You would open doors that no man can close and that You close doors no man can open. The doors that they pass through will always point them in the direction for the center of Your will for their lives. Father I ask that You give them favor with all they deal with and that many individuals will see the love of God in action.

For my prayer partners here at the workplace while many may be dealing with various tests in their lives, remind them that they are not alone. Jesus said in Matthew 18:19 (NKJV) "If two of you agree on earth concerning anything that they ask, it will be done for them by My Father in heaven." Therefore, I agree with them that the answer they seek is on the way. Yes, no or wait a while.

Thank You for allowing us to be busy with business.

Thank You for the favor we have with our customers and fellow employees. Help us to be instant in season with a Word of encouragement.

Father thank You for protecting our troops. Remind us that this is really a spiritual battle being fought in the flesh. I read the last chapter in the Bible and we WIN!!!!!!

Yang-Li

Prayer for Prosperity

Dear Heavenly Father,

Thank You for blessing us with the SUN! SON! The light always picks up our spirits and gives up hope and renewal of the spirit. We rejoice in the blessing of seeing the sun!

Today my prayers are for health and finances. All this week Lord, You have placed in my heart certain people to pray for. Therefore, I am praying for prosperity for **everyone** who reads this prayer. I petition it in the name of Jesus prosperity of health and wealth and a release from the bondage of woes that the enemy has used to suppress members of our families as well as ourselves.

I pray for a release of any strongholds and mercy from You for all our loved ones who have sinned against You. I pray for a nurturing relationship with You if they do not already have one.

I pray that any financial bonds that the enemy has against any of us will not prosper and be broken, allowing us the prosperity that we petition in the name of Jesus.

I pray Your healing hands touch those who are sick.

I pray for a gentle winter for those who can least afford the heating bill and for those left out in the cold.

I ask for forgiveness in our hearts and to love as Jesus loves.

I pray for the unspoken prayers that only You have heard, to be answered with Your mercy.

Finally, thank You Jesus for always loving us and going to the Father to intercede even though we are not worthy.

Amen

Ursula

Philippians 4:6 "Be anxious for nothing, but in everything by prayer..."

Prayer for Continuing Trust

Good morning Father,

How wonderful You are!

This time last year, many of us in this group were concerned about our jobs among other things and You have calmed our concerns even now and for that we thank You.

We trusted You then and we trust You now. Who else can we turn to for our daily needs but unto You Lord? You have never left us nor failed us in any matter great or small. Again, we thank You.

Continue to be our Lord and Savior and we will be Your people.

We truly thank You in the mighty name of Jesus,

Amen

Mike Taylor

Prayer for the Bereaved

Heavenly Father in the mighty name of Jesus,

How we worship you for all the great things you have done for us.

You have predestined each of us unto greatness and given us freewill to carry out our destiny in this earth which will later be expounded upon for all eternity.

There comes a time for us to depart from this world and move into a new and permanent season, which can be a bittersweet moment for some of us.

The bitterness of losing the presence and comfort of our loved one can be overwhelming until we remember the joy of the ever so sweet release that you have granted our loved one from the troubles of this world.

No more trials or temptations.
No more sorrow or aggravations.
No more sickness, no more ills.
No more taking 30,000 pills.
No more aching bones or any type of pain;
But of peace, tranquility and Godly gain.

Yes, we are overjoyed with the comfort of knowing that our loved one has found your rest.

Now Father, give peace and comfort to those of us who must remain in this world to carry on the Gospel; that great and honorable news of Jesus Christ.

Help the bereaving family to grieve in a healthy manner. Give them space to cry and shed their tears of times gone by in remembrance of those great and notable moments that were shared with the loved one.

After they have grieved sufficiently, give them a new and energetic heart for you to finish this race with the hope and assuredness of seeing your face and their loved one again.

In Jesus name - Amen

Mike Taylor

Prayer for Effective Witness

Good morning Dad,

Once again we come before You in prayer because of what Jesus did for us on Calvary's cross.

What a glorious day this is - simply because Your Holy Spirit has gone before us. With courage today, we will follow His leading as we go about our daily tasks.

As He brings across our paths those to whom we meet, help us to be instant in season with a word of encouragement to let them know just how good You are. The world is hurting and more than ever they need to see the real church - sons and daughters of the living God who truly represent You.

Help us not to be ashamed to be called children of God. As we live our life before mankind, help them to see Your love, joy and peace in us. Even in the midst of our personal challenges, let them see our trust in You so that their faith rises to meet Your abilities and that is when miracles will happen.

Guard our tongues so that we don't speak anything that is contrary to Your Word. Help us to speak life in every circumstance.

I lift up my fellow prayer partners today. While things may not be going the way they would like or if they are overwhelmed, I remind them "that all things work together for good to them that love God." We can't have a testimony without a test.

Remind them that they have already overcome because "greater is He that is in them than he that is in the world."

Thanks Dad, for pouring Your goodness on each and everyone, meeting every need and granting them the desire of their hearts as it aligns with Your plan for them.

Guide our leadership at the workplace. Always help them to keep their integrity. Protect our troops and bring them home safely. We pray for the peace of Jerusalem and ask that the leadership in our government will stand up and support her.

In Jesus Name, Amen

Wallace

James 5:16 - "The effective, fervent prayer of a righteous man..."

Prayer Against an Attack from the Enemy

Heavenly Father,

We thank You for all things as You know all things and provide all things.

We ask You to forgive us of our sins and help us to not sin against You. Hear and read our words then bless accordingly. We know You are faithful to forgive us and yet we shall not take Your forgiveness and mercy for granted.

Now that You have forgiven us, we come before You as a humble people on behalf of Lela. I looked up the meaning to the name Father and was delighted to discovered it means "Old wise one" and "God is gracious".

We know You are ancient and wise and most certainly gracious. We ask that You extend Your grace to Lela and heal her of this demonic affliction as it came on her quickly and from none other than the enemy.

We know even now that You have guided the doctor's hand with precision and yet we give You all of the praise.

I haven't heard of the outcome and yet I know what will come out. We come against this curse and this disease in the Mighty Name of Jesus!

The **Lord** rebuke this affliction in His might and power and release this family from this bondage as of this writing and forevermore.

We won't stop there, but we are petitioning You Father to open up the understanding over Lela and her entire family. If they don't know You and the pardoning of their sins then reveal Yourself unto them and receive them into Your flock.

Impress upon them how important it is to glorify You in all of their ways and then use each of them for Your Glory starting with Lela to her mother to the rest of the family. Let this family be known for their unselfish servitude unto You.

If You have found favor in me O' Lord, then please honor my words. I know I am not worthy and yet I still ask for this thing. You said in Your Word to ask and that You would do it and I know of a surety that You cannot lie; my prayer is not amiss as it is a good thing that **we** as a group ask of You.

With that being said, find favor in this group and receive the prayers that we submit to You. Because You are a righteous God, we know that You will judge accordingly and righteously and for that we truly thank You.

Meanwhile, we shall continue to praise You, sing unto You, honor You and pray in communion unto You in Jesus name this day and every day.

Amen

Mike Taylor

Corinthians 10:13 "There hath no temptation taken you..."

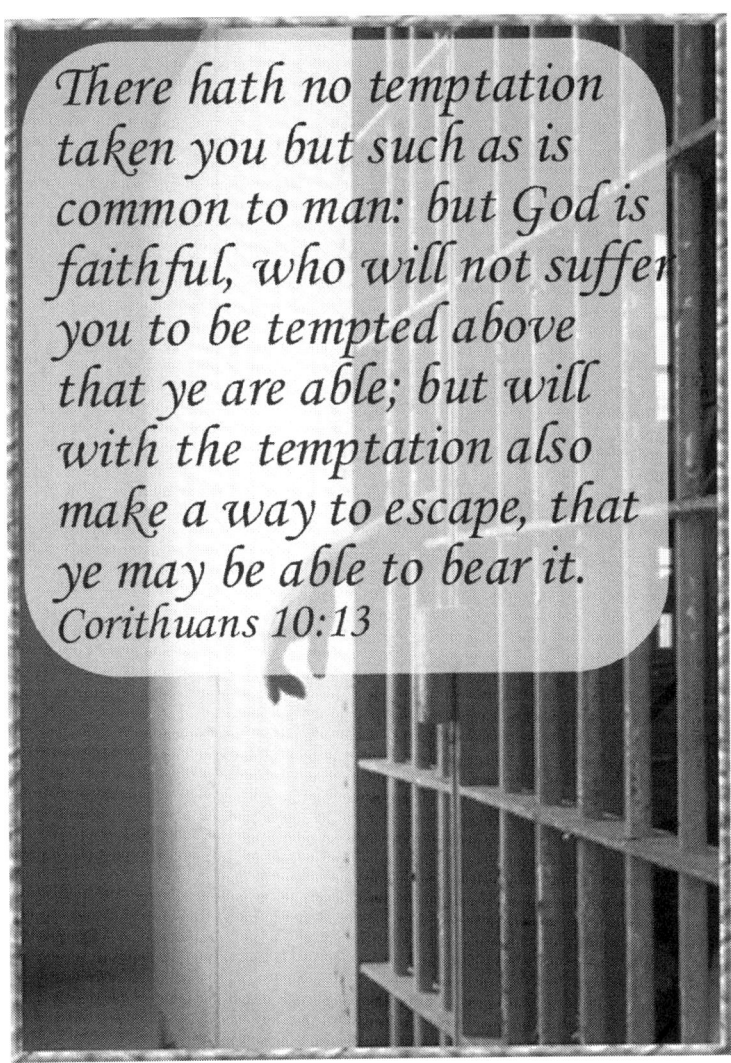

A Prayer for Weary Believers

How great Thou are!

You alone hold the world in your hands. Yet Father, You sent the Holy Spirit to dwell in our hearts because of what Jesus did for us on the cross.

You have declared to us that we are fearfully and wonderfully made. You know the very number of hairs on our head! How marvelous it is to know that the Creator of the universe knows me and cares about me. I shout from the roof top that **I am a child of God!**

Now today Father, I lift up the hands of my brothers and sisters, even as Aaron and Hur lifted up Moses' hands and ask that you bring them victory today.

Today if they should become weary in spiritual battles, remind them that the enemy is **defeated**; as the song says "Victory, Victory shall be mine. If I hold my peace and let the Lord fight my battle, Victory, Victory shall be mine."

We are Overcomers in the mighty name of Jesus. Thank You Father for what You are doing as You bring about Your perfect plan for each person who reads this prayer. Give them a greater measure of Grace as they wait on You. I ask for a peace that surpasses all of their human understanding so that, regardless of what their temporary circumstances are, those who know them will marvel at what the Lord has done.

In the sweet Name of Jesus,

Amen

Wallace

Psalms 30:5 "Weeping may endure for a night..."

Prayer in the Midst of Trouble

Good morning Father.

As David declared, "I will lift up my eyes to the hills; from whence comes my help? My help comes from the LORD, who made heaven and earth." Psalm 121:1-2 (NKJV)

If You had not helped us and been our strength O' Lord, where would we be? I simply thank You for all that You have done for us. Words alone cannot express our gratitude, therefore let our lives reflect Your goodness to us.

As those around us wonder why we are so happy in the midst of our trials (little do they know that You are changing us to be more like Jesus), give us the compassion and boldness to speak the truth in love that "Jesus is the answer" to their life situation as well as our own.

Encourage those who read this prayer **right now** with the knowledge that "nothing is impossible with God." I ask that You open the doors they are to go through and close those that they are not so that each one continues to walk towards the center of Your will.

Thank You Father for meeting all of their needs today, in Jesus Name and all God's people said,

"AMEN".

Teshia

Habakkuk 3:17 "Although the fig tree shall not blossom..."

Although the fig tree shall not blossom, neither shall fruit be in the vines; the labour of the olive shall fail, and the fields shall yield no meat; the flock shall be cut off from the fold, and there shall be no herd in the stalls: Yet I will rejoice in the LORD, I will joy in the God of my salvation.
Habakkuk 3: 17 - 18 KJV

Prayer for Perseverance

Good morning Father and praying partners,

What a glorious morning it is. Father, it dawned on me that we have recently closed another fiscal year and are still in business as proof of Your loving care. For we know that they prosper because of the praying agents You have place here for the good of the company and certainly for the good of the praying agents and their families.

In a couple of months, we will close out another calendar year and we are very grateful for how You have kept us through the thick and thin of it all. We will look back on this year and marvel at how You have brought us through and even now we know You are forever providing for our spiritual and natural necessities.

Because we know that You are faithful to Your Word, we ask that You continue to bless the members of this praying group and their families as well as those who are very close to them.

I pray a special blessing of release for a very special young salesman in body and soul. We are also looking forward to hearing some positive news about Lela.

I am thankful to have experienced the turmoil some of my brothers and sisters have went through these past months and to see how they stood fast in the Faith and in the Word, unmoveable. It solidifies the fact that I too can stand no matter what.

We shall continue to love one another today Father and again in action rather than words. Help us to choose our words wisely. Nonetheless, for those who may still be on the brink of total anxiety, give them peace of mind, heart and spirit as only You can. Heal the finances of those who need them healed in Jesus name.

Amen

Mike Taylor

Prayer for Enduring Personal Trials

Hi Ursula,

I am saddened to hear of your troubles, nonetheless; I am comforted in knowing that our Father has it all under control.

There must come a time when we throw our hands in the air and give it all to Father; I know and I have been there and still visit that situation from time to time. However, every time I am feeling low in spirit or unsure of my today let alone tomorrow, I still **make** myself happy and **make** myself smile through it all even if I can't remove the frowns of discomfort from my forehead; **I trust GOD!**

> *Heavenly Father, we come to you as humble servants before You asking for relief and release of the anguish that has overtaken my sister and Your daughter Ursula.*
>
> *You know of her situation completely and even now I suspect that You are working it out.*
>
> *Help Ursula to endure all that has befallen her whether from the enemy or from You as You grow her in Your kingdom.*
>
> *Help her to stay strong and not faint.*
>
> *Help her to realize that she cannot make anything happen and that everything she needs must come from You.*

Help her to separate herself from her immediate family spiritually, as painful as it may be so that You can commune with her on a level of her own.

*Help her to not feel alone because she is **not alone**.*

*Help her to realize that her help **is not coming from her sons or her husband, but from You alone.***

*Help her to understand that the $1200 or $1500 is not a show starter or stopper and that even if the offender should not return her money, the offender is not returning **Your** money and You will require the payment from his own head.*

We do pray that he return her money in full ($1500) and that You give Ursula a heart of peace and a mind to simply stand still to see how You will work out things in her life. Help Ursula to allow the men in her household to receive Your Word from You and others as they are either slow to receive it from Ursula or simply refuse to do so.

Remove the tears from hers eyes as You administer the vaccinations that will heal the men folk in her household no matter how painful it may be.

Send her to a quiet place where she can talk and commune with You, whether a local park or to a Christian retreat with other Christian women.

*Allow her to see **this day** that You are indeed working on her behalf and that You are still God, still her father and still in control of everything created yesterday today and tomorrow in the mighty name of Jesus!*

Amen

Be encouraged, Ursula for Father has heard your cry and seen your tears; He will give you peace.

Mike Taylor

Proverbs 12:4 "A virtuous woman is a crown to her husband"

Prayer that our Witnessing be Heard

Good morning Father,

What a glorious morning it is.

Kim prayed this morning from John 17:20-26 (NKJV). I will share that passage with our group as my prayer this morning.

****
Jesus Prays for All Believers

"My prayer is not for them alone. I pray also for those who will believe in me through their message, that all of them may be one, Father, just as you are in me and I am in you. May they also be in us so that the world may believe that you have sent me. I have given them the glory that You gave me, that they may be one as we are one— I in them and you in me—so that they may be brought to complete unity. Then the world will know that you sent me and have loved them even as you have loved me.

"Father, I want those you have given me to be with me where I am, and to see my glory, the glory you have given me because you loved me before the creation of the world.

"Righteous Father, though the world does not know you, I know you, and they know that you have sent me. I have made you known to them, and will continue to make you known in order that the love

you have for me may be in them and that I myself may be in them."

****

Father, thank You for Your loving spirit. Continue to be with us this day as You have been every day. For all that we need is in You and You have provided for us graciously in all that we need and want.

We shall continue to praise, honor and worship You out of our hearts with abundant love, for You alone are worthy!

Amen

Mike Taylor

Proverbs 30: 8 - 9 "Remove falsehood and lies far from..."

Prayer for Salvation

Partners,

There's an old school church song that sings:

"When I think of the goodness of Jesus and all he has done for me, my soul cries out Hallelujah! Thank God for saving me."

We echo those words today, for everything else pales to our soul salvation. I am truly thankful for how You watch over us and are always nearby.

Saturday, I was at the sports field sitting in the bleachers while waiting for our team to play. My young nephew who is about 5 years-old was tussling with a couple of boys who were a little older than him, but it was all in fun. A week earlier his cousin was harassing him when I came to his rescue. I told him if anyone ever bothered him to call on me and I will protect him.

Saturday, he remembered those words because when those boys got the best of him, he said "Uncle Mike, Save Me!" I was sitting in the bleaches about two benches above him and the boys. As soon as he said those words, those boys froze, took their hands off of him and looked at me with fear as I had a scowling look on my face from my thoughts, not because of the boys' play.

Nonetheless, it made me realize how much that situation was just like ours in the Spiritual. You are always right there to hear our cries and the enemy will certainly turn us loose when we do.

When we play, You are there.

When we work, You are there.

While we sleep, You are there.

Even though we may have trouble in our bodies at different stages whether physical or Spiritual, we know that You are in control and work all things for our good.

I pray that all is indeed well with my co-laborers in all areas of their lives; especially for their marriages as the enemy desires to upset the peace in the home and put family member against family member. Give them peace within the home and outside of the home.

Every time the enemy rears his ugly head against them, inspire them to witness or say something good about You to the next person they see.

We will glorify You Father for You are worthy to be lifted up before us. Again, we thank You for Your goodness and ask that You continue to be good toward us as we journey through this day.

As always. we shall continue to give You all honor, praise and glory both now and forever more in Jesus name.

Amen

Mike Taylor

Prayer for Honoring God

Heavenly Father,

How great it is to have such praying partners. Each prayer is anointed with power from on high and I ask for that same power to grasp each of us this day that we may exhibit Your character in our walk so that others will indeed inquire about our peculiar (good thing) nature.

I am constantly amazed at Your power in all aspects of our lives. Even the earth is subject to your power. Our nation or rather the East Coast is preparing for the appearance of a hurricane with all of its power and anger. As powerfully damaging as a hurricane can be, I marvel that You can simply speak a word to calm it.

You are truly the Awesome God! I wrote "the Awesome God" because there is only one God and that is You! You have not rendered unto us what we truly deserve and for that we thank You and with that being said, we ask for forgiveness of all of our sins and ask that You accept our very being as a living sacrifice for a sin offering.

Help us to make it through this day. If we should close our eyes on this world sometime, I pray that it is well with our soul. For it is our desire to exit this world in Your good grace for we do not wish to take You for granted as the children of Israel did, over and over again. Cleanse us, then use us for Your complete purpose and glory.

Meanwhile, we shall continue to give you all of the praise, honor and glory in Jesus name.

Amen

Mike Taylor

Psalms 73:25 - "Whom have I in heaven but you?"

Prayer for Men to Take Responsibility

What is man to You O' Lord that You should be so merciful? Who is man that would cause You to clothe Your only begotten Son in the suit of man's stink and to walk among us?

My Oh My! Heavenly Father, in the mighty name of Jesus I ask and implore You to forgive me of my sins and not hold them against me; please hear my prayer. There are some of us who do indeed strive to keep Your commandments and cherish Your Oracles to do them.

The enemy is fully aware of our desire and plight to resist him always. We are mere mortals and are no match whatsoever against the devourer as he is in the spirit world and we cannot fight what we cannot see; that is why we need You in all our ways to fight our battles.

My passion is to see my brothers and sisters with an emphasis on the men to remain strong in Your Word and unmovable. I realize that as they grow stronger, the enemy will try to derail their efforts as quickly and as often as he can; but thanks be to You Father that we have an advocate, a fighting chance and a battle plan that cannot fail.

Nonetheless Father, our adversary is a formidable foe and will not give up his fight against us just yet, as we will never give up our fight against him. While You have many strong women in the ministry, You have placed it in the hands of men and so many women have been thrust into the role of headship because many men won't assume their Godly appointment.

I am praying **right now** on behalf of our wonderful sisters who may or may not be in the leadership role in their home. Whether the head of a home is in the hands of a man or a woman, the enemy will attack those around them because he knows as Joe Frazier once said **"Kill the Body and the Head will die."**

He delights in creating discord in the household, in prayer groups, at work and even at church the most. He tries to have the women assume most of the leadership roles because he knows that is not Your divine order. You will not work in a knowingly out of order situation among the believers.

I recognize the need for encouragement, spiritual food, and power for one another. While I do understand the need to pray for other countries and our government leaders, it disturbs me to take my God-given resources such as prayer, words of encouragement, financial assistance, food, and imparting the Gospel to faraway places and then **my very neighbor (who is my brother and sister in Christ) is in need of these very things I write about!**

You know my passion, so why should I hide it? Your people, who are **right now** reading this prayer, need Your spiritual strength to get through this very day let alone the rest of this week. We do know that You hear us and that You will certainly provide for us in all things and we shall wait patiently while yet working earnestly.

Now concerning Your men; strengthen each of us to remain men of valor and Godly men in our walk and in all of our ways. Help us to assume and maintain our household as the head and not as dictators, but as wise men who can survey the surroundings and ensure that it is all pleasing to You and in order.

Help us to be as "MEN T.O.R.S., which stands for "Men Taking On Responsibilities Seriously." Help us all to **not** get weary of well doing, knowing that we shall indeed be rewarded handsomely if we faint not.

Finally Father, because I know nothing is too hard for You at all, I would like to ask for the safety and well being of Godly world leaders and that they will make Godly decisions to ease the burden of Your people.

Meanwhile we shall indeed give You all of the praise honor and Glory in the mighty name of Jesus Christ!

Amen-

Mike Taylor

Matthew 11:29 - 30 "Take my yoke upon you, and learn of me..."

Encouragement to Become a Virtuous Woman

My God, My God, My God!

I was just thinking about you for a couple of days, Teshia. How great it is to hear from you!

I have been praying that you have strong influences around you to help keep you strong and that you will not give up in your walk with Christ. I know that these times can be very trying and tempting to revert back to our own way in doing things. However, I am imploring you to just hold on and not be persuaded to do unsavory things.

Be wary of those around you who profess the name of Christ but are really wolves in sheep's clothing. They are miserable inside and try to make the Word of GOD in the name of Jesus of no effect in your life. They will try to justify their fake walk in Christ and rely on your lack of understanding in the bible as a key to manipulate you.

I am not necessarily speaking about anyone in particular there, but in general for people you see at work, home or the church you frequent.

The fact that you have been on my mind and that you have responded to my prayer is confirmation to me that you are warring inside and God has heard your cries. Your family needs a strong warrior; be that warrior and virtuous woman that God has called you to be.

If you feel lost or overwhelmed at times, go to God in your quiet time and tell him so. Tell him you don't know what to do or how to do it and that you desperately need his guidance. Ask him to forgive you of your sins. Ask him to help you to do good and not bad. Then, with God's help, do good and not bad. God will remove some of the bad people from you, but not all of them because some of them he will use to help make you stronger in your walk.

There will come a time when you will have to kiss your so-called friends goodbye. It will be painful, but worth it to cement your walk in Christ and to see the positive changes in your life and that of your children and grandchildren; for they are truly "Grand!"

Be encouraged! You are God's little princess and he loves you dearly.

Your servant in Christ,

Mike Taylor :)

Proverbs 31:10 "Who can find a virtuous woman?"

Prayer for those Abroad

Heavenly Father, in the name of Jesus:

How great You are and wonderful to behold. We give You honor and glory this day and everyday for You are worthy to be praised.

Thank You for keeping us thus far in our lives and for not giving up on any of us. Help us to continue in the gospel that You have placed before us. Be with each of us and help us to pull someone, anyone from the clutches of the enemy. Help us to examine ourselves so that You nor others will have to.

We pray that You protect our loved ones overseas and Christians throughout the world. We would not be upset if You make it so that we have great relief with the oil prices. Your Word says "We have not because we ask not" (not verbatim - James 4:2 NKJV) so we are asking for relief Father.

We trust You and thank You for all things in Jesus name.

Amen

Mike Taylor

Joshua 1:9 "Have I not commanded you?"

Prayer for the Strength of Friends

Heavenly Father, in the name of Jesus,

How sweet are the feet of those who carry Your Word and speak it proudly. How comforting it is to know (not **hope**) but to know someone is praying for you.

We all need the strength of fellowship even when we pray, for none of us are exempt from the attacks of the enemy. Now is the time for us to bond together to fight this spiritual war. It was the enemy who create the ploy of "divide and conquer" long before any general employed that tactic.

We will not allow him to divide Your people and with Your power and strength we shall overcome any obstacle that he put before us regardless of its nature for we have the scriptures as battle armor and in them we have our sword.

Reveal the enemy's camp and hiding places. Help each of us not to allow him to hide within us as thoughts of despair, dissension, or distrust beginning with **me**!

Help me to show forth Your **love**; the very love You have given me by putting my brothers and sisters in Christ ahead of my own welfare; by doing so, I am assured that You will be pleased and will look kindly upon me.

If I cannot change the hearts of men with Your Words coupled with the kindness of my actions then help me to not get weary of doing good and to continue in the fight because I believe Your Word when it says "We shall **reap** if we **faint** not." For we know You are able to complete this work that You started in us unto the day of Christ.

Now if there be any animosities, hurt feelings or unforgiveness in our group that the enemy will most certainly try to slip in among us, help each of us to:

* Truly shake it off.

* Truly put it behind us.

* Truly forgive one another as though it had never happened.

For we "**truly**" know this will please You and it will empower us to be an effective and powerful group of believers.

How can I effectively pray for the house of others (Israel and or my neighbor) when my own house is in disarray?

Thank You Father for each member of this group; we are many names, but one body and one spirit. If one should become weak, we who are strong will help to strengthen the weak with words of kindness, encouragement and with our natural resources when necessary in knowing that the same will support and comfort us.

You have set Your power on this group Father and for that we "**truly, truly, truly**" thank You and will not drop the ball.

Meanwhile, we shall fast and sing praises unto You for all that You've done, are doing and will do for us now and in the very near future.

Now unto You who is able to keep us focused and to keep us from falling when it is so convenient to fall; unto You who is able to present us without blame unto our Father; unto the only wise God our Father in the mighty name of Jesus, we all say "Amen, Amen and Amen!

Mike Taylor

Matthew 18:20 "For where two or three are gathered together..."

Prayer for Security in God

Dear Father,

Recently, we mourned for the loss of so many innocent lives and a tragedy that forever changed our nation and our safety. The effect afterwards was an outpouring of love to one another as we all realized how truly vulnerable we are. There is no safety in numbers.

Many years later, although we realized our safety is never going to be what it once was, we do realize that You, God and Father, are our sanctuary. For perils in life that are beyond our control, we know that we can cry out to You for comfort. I pray today Heavenly Father for our nation to come back to You and that our leaders of this country will come to You for wisdom.

So many are out of work, homeless and have lost everything for one reason or another. Please give them comfort and the ability to rebuild, find jobs, and to know You are God through Jesus Christ our Lord. Use Your people for an outpouring of love.

Financially so many are struggling in these hard times, please give our government leaders **wisdom** to help the poor and middle class to be able to afford gas, food and housing. So many people are walking away from their homes because they can't afford to live there anymore. We petition as the children of God for our prosperity and thank You for it now.

For new endeavors, I am praying for these ideas to become a source of financial prosperity for the people in this prayer group and for those reading this prayer **right now**. I pray that it would be just the beginning of a new prosperous wealth source to be used for Your Good and Your Glory.

Regarding unspoken prayers; please honor them Father for Your people as we move forward in our lives.

We give thanks and praise and honor to our loving Father as our eyes look up to You for guidance.

Amen

Ursula

Prayer for Unity

Father,

We humble ourselves before You. We confess both known and unknown sins before You. Thanking You for Your forgetfulness regarding them. You chose not to remember them. As Your body here on earth, we glorify You for what You are doing through us.

Dad, You see the challenges we are going through.

* Severe weather
* Destruction
* Demonic influences and the list goes on and on.

I believe the earth has the beginning of birth pains as it longs for its' Creator to return.

Now, more than ever we need Your children to be in unity. Help us to set aside the man interpreted ideas of Your Word. Our purpose is to share Your love found in a personal relationship with the LORD Jesus Christ.

We must begin Father by caring for each other. Accepting our brothers and sisters as they are, flaws and all. Jesus said "by this **shall** all men know you are my disciples that you love one another." So let it begin with me.

When my brothers and sisters are hurting I am

hurting, when they rejoice, I rejoice. We should be the first to lend an ear when they need a friend to listen. Maybe not to offer advice but to have a shoulder to lean on.

Thank You for Your strength today for the task ahead. I ask that You reveal Yourself in the little things that happen today.

Encourage your people hearts; reminding them that You are with them every step of the way. Bless them on their jobs. Give them favor with their fellow workers, bosses and customers.

I ask that You continue to guide our leadership here at the workplace. Give them favor in the business transactions.

Protect our troops and bring them home safely. For those who paid the ultimate sacrifice I pray they were ready to meet You.

I pray for the peace of Israel. In the sweet Name above all names the Name of Jesus.

Amen,

Wallace

Prayer and Advice Concerning Marriage Infidelity

My Dear Marlita,

This is a long post, so settle back with a hot beverage.

My name is Mike Taylor; I am Kim's husband.

Kim is grieving over your plight and has shared your story with me so that I could join her in effective prayer for and with you.

Please join me in this prayer to God:

> *Heavenly Father, in the mighty name of Jesus; we come before you as a humble people asking you for forgiveness of all of our sins before You. We know we have missed the mark on several occasions and we are not excusing ourselves. We are asking You for help in leading and guiding us unto all truth in the way we should move in the natural and most certainly the spiritual.*
>
> *Now, we breathe deeply (take a deep breath Marlita). We thank you for Your forgiveness because we know You are faithful to forgive us. Now that You have forgiven us, again we breathe deeply (take another deep breath); such a sweet release from our troubles.*
>
> *Hear now this prayer Father, on behalf of Marlita. You have read the words she has*

written and even now "I" know for sure You are working on her behalf whether it is good or not so good in her eyes. Help her to see that You have a calling on her life that no one but she can accomplish and that if she will just endure for a little while, You will show Yourself in a majestic way to her.

In the meantime, comfort her heart and soul as only You can. Either ease her heart of pain or help her to endure.

I know that what the enemy means for bad, You mean for good and You have already won, which means Marlita wins as well.

***No man** loves their children as much as You love Yours. **No man** can care for his children in the majestic way You care for Yours. **No man** has endured the hurt by his children for as long and as hard as You have endured the hurt and distrust of Yours.*

That is just one of many reasons why we love and honor You even now in spite of whatever we are going through.

I know it pains You deeply to see Marlita in such pain and grief especially since You know it is Your arch enemy behind it and the only reason he is behind it is because You know what it takes to strengthen Marlita for the journey and task(s) You have for her AND quite possibly her husband.

*With that being said, open up the heart and mind of her husband completely as only You can. Give him a lucid moment where he will question his own actions and ways. Give him a heart of love for You first and foremost, then a completely pure heart for his sweet wife, Marlita. Let there be peace in their household even now. Move on her husband **"right now"** in the name of Jesus with a spirit of discomfort in the things he may be doing which are not like you and that are oppressive to Marlita.*

Give Marlita a mind to forgive her husband. I said mind as oppose to heart because if she has a mind to forgive her husband and do it, You will be glorified because she will have made the choice to forgive him for the love she has for You more than her husband.

Heal this marriage as I know You will. Unite this couple in such a way that those around them will come to them for counsel as You will prescribe.

In the meantime, we will continue to give You all the honor and praise in the mighty, mighty name of Jesus.

Amen and again I say Amen!

Now then my dear sister, here comes a strong critique from a humble servant of God as these are my observations as God's Holy Spirit placed it on my heart.

Why are you in such shock? It is time to come out of shock. No more are you to be the "shockee" but rather the "shocker"; are you up to that **first** task?

It is good that you act as if everything is OK because everything is OK in Christ if you choose to believe it; **do you believe it?**

Why are you disappointed with yourself? Are you sinning openly before God? Don't you understand that we (me certainly included) are absolutely nothing of ourselves and it is only by God's good grace and mercies that we breathe?

Grace is receiving good things from God that we **do not deserve at all**, while Mercy is **not receiving the punishment that each of us truly deserve, period!**

You should be very, very happy about yourself and your life because you have the Lord; you do have the Lord, don't you? You do believe in Him and trust Him, don't you? Because for God to move on your behalf you must first believe in Him and believe that He is indeed a rewarder to those that truly seek after Him and not of themselves.

You are right when you say: "**Only the Lord knows where I am in truth and how I'm seeing myself.**" That is why I have written these words as God has placed on my heart; will you receive them? You must let your anger rest on God. OK, let me say that again. God and I know it is a difficult thing for you to do but even so, you must let your anger rest on God's shoulders as painful as that might be; He wants you to so that He can show you just how powerful He is and how much He loves you.

As long as your husband is not physically hurting you, please stand for God. Do you read your bible? If so, then think on things of God in times of trouble. Think on pure things, on lovely things, on happy times and Godly things. Sing a song of praise to God even when you don't feel like it and are hurting deeply inside. When you deny yourself in this manner and this manner alone is when God stands up from his throne and says something like:

> *"Hold up, hold up! Wait one cotton-picking minute! My baby, Marlita is down there singing me a love song. Even while she is hurting inside and out, she is singing to me!*
>
> *Now, I know the world is troubling. I know about the oil spill in the gulf. I know about the unrest in the Middle East. I know of the oppression that Israel is experiencing **right now**.*
>
> *I know how bad the economy is, but my baby girl is singing through her troubles and unto me, so I've got to move on her behalf **right now!**"*

Can't you see, Dear Sister, that you mean a lot to God? Your husband seems depressed because God, I said God, is working on him **right now** and that is what you want. Just like only God knows where you are at in truth and how you see yourself; only He knows where your husband is at and how he sees himself.

Has it even dawned on you that your husband is torn on trying to do the right thing and that his flesh is warring with him inwardly? Our flesh is a formidable foe and only God can defeat it. It is your flesh that causes you to not want to forgive your husband and want to stay angry with him for hurting you. Your flesh wants him to hurt like you have hurt and then you feel sad when/ if he does because your good Spirit knows that God would rather there be peace and love between the two of you as it must be for the two of you to have a working relationship with God.

You said: "*I'm trying to think what is good about myself, but in my heart I feel otherwise.*" OK sweetie, here comes an eye opener or revelation. There is absolutely no good in you, me, Kim or anyone else. **Only God is good** and that is from the bible! See Matthew 19:17, Psalms 14:3, Romans 3:10.

As soon as you come to realize that, your life and lifestyle will immediately change for the better.

Your mind is weak because you have not allowed God to renew it in Him. Remember He said to let this mind be in **you** which was also in Christ Jesus (Philippians 2:5). As long as we try to do things our way, it will come to nothing.

If you are indeed a child of the King, the one and only true God, then you are a princess and need not worry over simple things. God will supply your needs and provide you with your wants, but you must trust and believe.

Again, you are worth more than all the treasures of the earth to God, but it means nothing if you don't believe it.

Until you can get past this minor setback in your life, God's plans for you remain on hold and others will miss out on great blessings and opportunities because God's little Marlita is still crying.

This part are my words and not those of God: There are a lot of women who are just as strong as or stronger than men who God will use because the men around them won't step up. However when they do step up, then God will allow those women to relax and breathe comfortably, while the men be men. You really are one of those strong women who God wants to use, but you just needed to hear it from a stranger who is really a brother to you and a servant to God.

Will you now become that strong woman for Christ until God moves your husband into his rightful place in your household so that the two of you can go ahead and get started with the ministry that God has planned for you two?

I have asked a lot of questions here. You should isolate them and answer each one to yourself for I don't need your answer, but God does.

Will you answer the call?

I pray that God continue to bless you and your husband, dear sister.

Your servant in Christ,

Mike Taylor

Ruth 3:11 - "And now, my daughter, fear not..."

Prayer to Forgive Family Member Theft

Good morning prayer partners,

I pray to Father that we all be released of personal oppressions and that we prosper as our soul prospers.

I pray that we truly forgive all past hurts and move forward in a positive and productive manner that will give us peace and peace to those around us daily whereby we glorify our Father in Heaven.

I have petitioned this prayer for you because of the release of pain I have just experienced and I hope that by sharing this, it will bless your souls and encourage you to do the same.

Sometime last year as I was preparing to make my move out of state, I noticed that a large number of my DVDs were removed from my household. Some of the DVDs were taken case and all, while others were just removed from the case and the cases were left behind in an effort to avoid suspicion.

I was livid! I quickly deduced that the culprit was one of my family members who had visited my home while my mother, who was in her declining months of life, was living with me under my care.

I even thought back to when it might have happened, which would have been while I was at work and my mother was taking a bath, which would have allowed my family member time to do what they would.

This particular family member has a history of stealing from the family, which is why I was very leery of having them at my home while I was away, but for the sake of my mother I allowed it to be so. Again, I didn't realize the theft until my move as I didn't have time to view my collection back then.

I never confronted the family member, but I did mention it to other members in my family. I told the other members in my family that I forgave that particular family member and I would just let it go. However, I could not let it go easily because every time I thought about viewing an old classic, the blood would burn hot in my veins and I would tell myself that it was OK and I forgave my family member.

Finally, the Lord our Father spoke to my heart and said "If you truly forgave them, then tell them so that they and you both know, then **truly** move on!"

After over a year of believing that I had forgiven my family member, I made it official on a Sunday and called them. They received my call and my soul was totally flushed of all past hurt and it felt so good. I feel as though I can move to an even higher plane in God because even though I felt I had forgiven my family member spiritually, I had to manifest it in the natural by **saying it to them** for all to see and hear; especially my family. My continued silence would have been a great weapon for the enemy to use against them, me and those around us but now that weapon has been removed from his arsenal and thanks be to GOD!

So again, I encourage you to forgive those who spitefully use you and go to them in forgiveness and seeking forgiveness if that is the case **as GOD directs you!**

You guys are **constantly** in our prayers and we love each of you very much!

To GOD be the Glory!!!

Your servant in Christ,

Mike Taylor

Phillipians 4:7 "...And the peace of God, which surpasses all understanding..."

Prayer for Favor in Court

Hey Ursula,

Rather than pray for Josh's court situation next week, we will thank Father for the outcome both now and on the date.

With that being said:

> *"Because You know all Father, we thank You **right now** in the name of Jesus for handling "our" son Josh's situation and truly honor You for not giving up on him and on us as a whole and as individuals. You are truly an awesomely incredible Father and we love You dearly because You are and have been so **great** to us.*
>
> *I was just reading in Judges where You told Israel to call on the gods of the Ammonites or whatever people were oppressing them at the time to deliver them because You delivered them from the hands of the Egyptians and such. However, as You watched them suffer, the Bible said Your soul could not take it any longer and with Your compassionate heart You delivered them from the turmoil that they brought on themselves.*
>
> *This is why we praise and thank You now because we are confident that whatever happens on Josh's court date will be for the*

ultimate good of Josh and his parents and we stand firm on that notion.

So allow us to say thank You and say Hallelujah in advance and again on the day of his court appearance as You perform Your wondrous work on our behalf for You alone are GOD!"

With all our love,

Mike Taylor

Isaiah 54:17 "No weapon that is formed against thee shall prosper..."

Prayer for Spiritual Change

Good morning, Great Father, for You are **great**!

How we thank You in all our ways because You are merciful and Your mercies endures forever.

I recognize Your special protection on behalf of the prayers that have been sent to You on my behalf at the request of others. I thank You and my brothers and sisters in Christ for the love they have for me.

I am asking that You bless each one in this prayer group tremendously in the spiritual and natural for their unselfish prayers toward others both near and far. I am also asking that others will adapt to the Godly character that they exemplify. It's is easy to adapt to Your surroundings, which is why we ask that You surround us daily.

As You know Father, Kim and I golf on Tuesdays. This past Tuesday, the temperature was about 36 degrees with a light drizzle of rain. I truly thank You for the rain as we have been in a two to three month drought.

The interesting thing about Tuesday's weather, Father, is that a year ago at this time I would have welcomed that weather for golfing because I would essentially have had the course to myself. However, as soon as I stepped out of our front door, I quickly turned around and told Kim we were not going because it was "too cold"!

Then I realized that I have become somewhat accustomed to my surroundings and can no longer tolerate temperatures of certain degrees because I am in a new region.

That is why we clamor around You and can no longer tolerate a sinful lifestyle because we dwell in a new atmosphere and new surroundings that we fully enjoy.

Help us to not wander dear Lord and continue to strengthen us this day and every day.

Meanwhile we shall continue to give You all the praise honor and Glory in the mighty name of Jesus!

Amen

Mike Taylor

Encouragement: Seek the "Son" and Live!

Good morning precious Father,

Your smile indeed covers the sky and we pray that you constantly smile on us.

As Kim was watering our tomato plants one day, we were amazed to see that although the plants were planted out of the bottom of the pots and hung upside down, the stems started to instinctively turn upwards to seek the "sun."

The tomato plants **knew** that only by seeking the "sun" could they find the nourishment they needed to grow and reach their maximum potential.

Similarly, we also know to seek the "SON" everyday so that we can grow "Upwards" and become all that God would have us to be.

We witnessed another amazing thing with the plants. In Kim's effort to thread the plants through the opening at the bottom of the basket, she broke the main stem of one of them; not completely severed, but greatly damaged.

Instead of discarding the plant we decided to leave it alone in hope that somehow it might repair itself, but we were fully expecting it to wither and die.

The amazing thing is that it brought forth flowers just like the other plants in the same basket which had not been broken. Even more amazing is that it had also brought forth **six tomatoes**. The plants that were **not broken** had only brought forth flowers but **"no fruit!"**

This situation reminded me that God desires for us to bear fruit in our lives, which is a natural outgrowth of our relationship with him. In order to bear fruit, we must be broken. We must recognize our weaknesses and hurts and bring them to God so that He can heal them; He is the only one who can!

If we insist on being prideful, pretending that everything is AOK and deny our need for God, we might look good to others on the outside with our pretty flowers, but we will never bear fruit. The fruit in our lives is something tangible that others can taste and see that the Lord is Good!

I pray that you receive these words in your heart and that they will inspire you to bring your brokenness to God. Let him heal you as you bask in the "SON'S" light so that you can bring forth an abundance of fruit that others can see and taste in the mighty name of Jesus.

Father, we are truly relying on you to bring all good and great things alive in our life and we thank you for them **right now** in the mighty, mighty name of Jesus.

Amen

Mike Taylor

1 Chronicles 16:34 "O give thanks unto the Lord; for he is good..."

Encouragement: Fighting a Troubling Spirit

From a brother in Christ who was warring within himself, but got things right

Good morning, Men of God!

Men, I would like to take this time to give my sincere apology for any hurt or wrong any of you feel that I've done to you.

I want you to know that I've been troubled in my spirit and have allowed myself to feel negatively toward some of you.

They that I have had issues with, I have approached, talked with heart-to-heart and have apologized personally.

It is never my desire to sow discord among the brothers. I do have a genuine love and desire to see each of you in the place and operating in gifts that God has ordained for and has given you. I have felt recently that satan has had a hold of me and the only way to break that hold was to exploit his device.

Men, I believe in being sincere in this life. There's a whole lot we can hide from one another, but everything is naked and open before Him which we have to do. It is my advice to any of you who may be going through anything remotely close or similar to do whatever you need to do to get free.

The battle within oneself can be destructive if it isn't dealt with accordingly in a timely manner. Don't worry about what man has to say about you getting right with God and others. God, Himself is the only one who can judge you.

Please, know that I love each of you and it is my prayer that we move forward in unison and oneness.

Sincerely,

Yosef

****

Praise Father continually Yosef,

Your action is to be commended and it's a very effective approach to fight against our common enemy whose name I don't like to say or even type.

I have been with our group for just over a year and I have enjoyed a very strong and Godly bond with the brothers.

I have observed how the brothers come together and have seen the power and anointing of our Father in Heaven over the brotherhood.

I have been blessed spiritually by you and so many

others in this group. We have a great shepherd and I have watched him and saw how great his love is for God's people and it moved me greatly. We have an incredible and powerful group of **men** willing to perform the unadulterated Word of **God**!

Our common enemy have also seen all of this and has purposed and dispatched agents to try and disrupt this great thing that Father has begun in us all.

But thanks be to our Father in heaven that we are Overcomers and we shall prevail in all areas of our walk in and with Christ.

I feel confident that this proactive approach you have taken will only add to the power we already possess from on high and it will only make us stronger in Christ.

Be at peace my brother, take a deep leisurely breath and we the brothers of this group will breathe with you and lift you up as you have been doing for us.

Your servant in Christ,

Mike Taylor

Encouragement: It Will Get Better

Father what a privilege You have given to us to partner together and pray. Knowing the promise of Jesus to us that "where two or three agree on touching anything," we thank You for the answer to our prayers throughout this past year.

While we continue to wait for Your will to be accomplished, we thank You for Your grace that has held us together. We thank You for the healings, financial blessings, restored relationships just to name a few.

Father as we look upon the time we are living in we anticipate the return of Jesus soon. Father, we still have loved ones that don't know Jesus. We free Your Holy Spirit to do whatever it takes to bring them to the saving knowledge of Jesus just as You did with Saul who became Your servant Paul.

Help us to remember that You have a plan for us that fits into Your perfect will. Help us rekindle the fire to hunger for You so that our lives are a great book that can be read of all men.

Father I speak Your blessings over each partner. Remind them they are royalty for we are children of the most high God.

We reign with the King of Kings; so Father when the devil reminds us of our past we shall remind him of his future.

Amen

Ursula

Encouragement: Your Turn to Love God

Great morning O Father in heaven.

You created Abraham and he loved You.

Time moved on and You created Isaac and he loved You.

Time moved on and You created David and he loved You.

Time moved on and You created so many more souls who loved You.

Now O' Lord, You have set aside this time frame for us; as it is our turn to love You. When we think of the quadrillion-billion-millions of zillion people times 10 that You have created to love You and to receive an eternal gift of love, we are in awe to be counted in that number for we are not worthy Lord and yet here we are counted among the blessed.

How can I petition You for anything when You have done so much for us already.

Nonetheless, I ask that You continue to be our God and guide us unto all truth and we shall be Your faithful servants with much love in Jesus name.

Amen

Mike Taylor

READER:

Take a moment "**Right Now**" to praise and thank God openly if you can or worship him silently.

Matthew 18:3 "Except ye be converted, and become as little children..."

Pray as our Father in Heaven Instructs: He Knows all Things

We honor You today, Father in Heaven, for all that You have done for us. We ask You to forgive us of our sins and help us to not sin against You.

As we prepare to enter into the last month of this year, help us to plan an agenda according to Your will that will promote the Gospel and bring You Glory so that we may leave this month with much spiritual gain and enter the new year with much expectation.

I pray that You will be with each one in this praying group and bless accordingly. I pray a special prayer my Christian brothers and sisters for whatever they may need or may be going through; whether spiritual or natural, I am asking that You grant their requests in a mighty way. Let there be peace for them at work and at home - especially at work.

For You alone are God all by Yourself and we all stand naked before You, hiding nothing. So be with us this month and every month, this holiday season and beyond.

Meanwhile, we will certainly give You all the praise honor and glory in the mighty name of Jesus.

Amen.

Mike Taylor

Isaiah 26:3 "Thou wilt keep him in perfect peace..."

Prayer for the Preparation of Christ's Return

Father - Good morning.

We thank You that Your Spirit, Your sweet Holy Spirit is with us today.

Jesus said that "He when the Spirit of truth shall come, He will guide us into all truth (John 16:13)." Because of that promise we **will** not be deceived by the enemy. "For all the promises of God are yea and amen in Christ Jesus (2 Corinthians 1:20)."

The promise I speak over this prayer group this morning, Father is "peace." Psalm 119:165 says "great peace have those that love thy law and nothing shall by any means offend them."

How wonderful to know that regardless of the temporary circumstance, the unkind word spoken, or relational problem that we are dealing with, it will have no impact on how we react knowing that You Father have it under control. We ask for Your grace as You work all things for Your good in our lives.

Another week has come and gone, which reminds us that we are that much closer to the return of Jesus. Help us to remember not to be weighed down with the cares of this world. Help us to live as if the next moment we would be in Your presence for all eternity.

I thank You Father for Your blessings on my brothers and sisters here at the workplace. Help us to work with integrity, honoring You. Guard our mouths so that we only speak life.

Father, help us to be a people that when the world is hurting we are the first ones they run to for prayer. Not because we are special but because they know we serve an awesome GOD!!!!!!

Thank You Father for blessings our place of employment with constant business. Continue to guide our leadership with Biblical truths in business which is quality, honesty, fair value and dependability.

Thank You for watching over our troops. I ask that You give our President wisdom and ask that You surround him with Godly men and women who honor and serve You.

We pray for peace in Jesus Name,

Amen

Wallace

About the Author and my Healing Testimonies

If you came to this page to read something about me, well this page is not about me, but rather **About the TRUE Author of this book.**

Of course you probably know I am talking about God in the name of Jesus who is **the author and finisher of our faith and this book.**

He is the One who has made this book possible.

He is the One who has forgiven me of my sins, more times than I can remember.

He is the One who has healed my body miraculously on two different occasions.

I shall indeed share with you those two miraculous healings:

The first miraculous healing was in the early 2000's. I had a horrific back problem which caused me great pain. From a profile view, I looked straight but from a frontal view, my body would literally turn or rather curve to the left. I had been seeing my doctor for just a tightness in my back before this turn of events (hmm, a little pun in there), but then it just got progressively worse.

One night at bible study, God placed it on the Pastor's heart to call people up for healing so that he could pray for each one individually. I should have gone, but I allowed the enemy to convince me that if many people came up, we would be there all night. So I didn't go up and it would have served me right if God had never healed me.

Nonetheless and thanks be to God that He is a merciful and forgiving God. As I laid in my bed that night while watching T.V. I shifted and felt three small pops in my back which I thought nothing of. The next day I got up to shower and didn't realize that I was turning and bending with no pain whatsoever. Then it dawned on me that I felt no pain and I started to twist and move about every which way.

However the final observation came when I hastily went to look at myself in the mirror and saw that I was standing straight in my profile and frontal view and I stand that way today--- To God be the Glory!

~

The second miraculous healing was on Wednesday December 7, 2011. I had suffered a rotator cuff injury in my right shoulder. Again, I was in great pain and hid it from my wife for as long as I could. I could not lift my right arm to a horizontal plane without great pain and certainly could not lift it over my head.

Being self-employed, my wife and I could not afford health insurance. As it was, we were having a night of fasting and prayer in lieu of bible study when my Pastor suddenly said "There's a healing at the altar.

If you are in need of a healing, come up to the alter now for your healing."

Now, I started to get off my knees to go, but then changed my mind to stay and pray. Then, I changed it again and went because I knew I needed a healing and could ill afford to go to a doctor plus, I remembered the back repair healing of years gone by.

As the Pastor moved down the aisle touching and anointing the people and long before he got to me, God spoke to my mind and said "Move your arm." I rolled my shoulder gingerly and noticed it was sore but not painful so I moved it a little more aggressively, then I swung it this way and that way and I lifted it over my head and straight into the air as if I was trying to reach God.

Once I was finished "waving my arm in the air like I just didn't care", I sat down because I was healed and did not need a touch from man because I had already been touched and healed by God personally.

I followed up by testifying to the healing the following Sunday because I didn't want my sudden exit from the healing line to be misconstrued as something negative and it gave me another chance to glorify God openly.

Once again, to God be the Glory!

Personal Journal of Testimonies (JOT)

When God answers your personal prayers, it is a good idea to write down what He did for you. You will have a record of answered prayers so that when your faith is low, you can strengthen it once again through reading your victory stories.

Made in the USA
Lexington, KY
15 September 2015